I0021471

GO INCOGNITO

Your Essential Guide To Online Anonymity

anon.ym

anon.ym

CONTENTS

Go Incognito: Your Essential Guide To Online Anonymity

Introduction

Introduction to Online Anonymity

In today's digital age, online activity leaves a trail. Websites track our clicks, social media platforms mine our data, and governments monitor our communications. This erosion of privacy fuels the desire for online anonymity, a shield to protect our identities and navigate the digital landscape with freedom.

Forget the myth of "online anonymity" as a passive state. This book is your active manual, empowering you to break free from the shackles of digital surveillance. We'll peel back the layers of the digital surveillance, exposing the hidden mechanisms that track and profile you. You'll learn how to unmask yourself from the prying eyes of corporations, governments, and even nosy neighbors.

Go Incognito is more than just a technical manual. It's a manifesto for digital freedom. We'll explore the ethical implications of online anonymity, debunk common myths, and equip you with the tools and techniques to confidently navigate the digital landscape without sacrificing your privacy.

This eBook explores the practical applications of online anonymity through real-world case studies. We'll delve into diverse scenarios where anonymity empowers individuals and collectives, from whistleblowing and activism to creative expression and personal safety.

Within these pages, you'll discover:

- The Five Pillars of Online Anonymity: Master the essential principles that underpin true invisibility in the digital world.
- Tools of the Trade: From privacy-focused browsers and encrypted messaging apps to anonymizing networks and advanced data protection techniques, we'll equip you with the arsenal to stay hidden.
- Beyond the Tech: Understand the social and psychological aspects of online anonymity, learn how to manage your online persona, and navigate the challenges of staying "off the grid."
- Real-world Scenarios: Put your newfound knowledge into action with practical guides for anonymizing your online activities, from browsing the web to social media and financial transactions.

Go Incognito is not just a guide; it's a call to action. It's time to reclaim your privacy, protect your identity, and experience the digital world on your own terms. So, grab your digital mask and dive into this essential guide. The power to vanish online is yours.

Ready to disappear? Let's go incognito.

CHAPTER 1
UNDERSTANDING ONLINE ANONYMITY

Understanding Online Anonymity

In a world increasingly defined by digital footprints, the allure of online anonymity is undeniable. But what exactly does it mean to be anonymous online, and why might someone choose to shed their digital skin.

I. Threats to Privacy in the Digital Age:

- Data Breaches: Our personal information, from financial records to social media posts, is constantly stored and transmitted online, making it vulnerable to hackers and data breaches. These breaches can have devastating consequences, including identity theft, financial loss, and reputational damage.
- Surveillance: Governments and corporations alike are increasingly collecting vast amounts of data on our online activities. This data can be used to track our movements, monitor our communications, and even predict our behavior.
- Tracking: Seemingly innocuous cookies and trackers follow us across the web, creating detailed profiles of our interests, purchases, and online habits. This information can be used for targeted advertising, manipulation, and even discrimination.

II. Benefits of Online Anonymity:

- <u>Security</u>: In an age of cybercrime, online anonymity can offer a layer of protection against identity theft, financial scams, and online harassment.
- <u>Freedom of Expression</u>: Anonymity can empower individuals to express themselves freely, without fear of censorship, retaliation, or discrimination. This is particularly important for those living in oppressive regimes or facing societal pressures.
- <u>Avoiding Discrimination</u>: Anonymity can level the playing field, allowing individuals to be judged based on their ideas and contributions, rather than their race, gender, or other personal characteristics.

III. Myths and Misconceptions about Online Anonymity:

- Myth: Being anonymous online means being invisible and untraceable.
- Reality: While complete anonymity is difficult to achieve, various techniques and tools can significantly enhance online privacy and make it more challenging to track individual users.
- Myth: Only criminals and bad actors care about online anonymity.
- Reality: Everyone has the right to privacy and control over their online data. Anonymity can be a valuable tool for protecting oneself from harm and discrimination in the digital age.

- Myth: Anonymity online means never using social media or sharing personal information.
- Reality: Maintaining a healthy balance between anonymity and online engagement is possible. Individuals can choose to share specific information with trusted communities while remaining anonymous to the broader public.

Understanding the motivations and benefits of online anonymity is crucial in navigating the complex landscape of our digital lives. By recognizing the threats to privacy and the value of anonymity, we can make informed choices about how to protect ourselves and exercise our right to freedom of expression online.

CHAPTER 2
THE LAYERS OF ONLINE IDENTITY

The Layers of Online Identity

I. unmasking your digital footprint:

our online identity isn't just a username and profile picture. It's a complex tapestry woven from various threads, each revealing a piece of our digital persona. Understanding these layers is crucial for navigating the online world with awareness and safeguarding our privacy.

Layer 1: The Surface We Present

I. <u>IP Address and Location Tracking</u>

The first layer, the one we willingly share, is our IP address and location. Every time we connect to the internet, our device leaves a digital footprint in the form of a unique identifier. This IP address can be used to pinpoint our approximate location, often to the city or even neighborhood level. While some services require location data for functionality, others can exploit it for targeted advertising or even surveillance.

Layer 2: The Fingerprints We Leave

II. <u>Browser Fingerprinting and Online Activity Monitoring</u>

Moving deeper, we encounter browser fingerprinting, a technique that gathers unique characteristics of our device and browsing behavior. From the fonts our browser supports to the screen resolution and plugins we use, these details create a digital fingerprint that can be surprisingly accurate in identifying us across different websites and platforms. Additionally, online activity monitoring tracks our clicks, searches, and interactions, further enriching the data profile associated with our identity.

Layer 3: The Social Echo Chamber

III. Social Media Footprint and Digital Breadcrumbs

Our social media presence forms another crucial layer of our online identity. The posts we share, the pages we like, and the people we connect with paint a picture of our interests, values, and even social circles. This digital footprint can be surprisingly revealing, offering insights into our personalities and activities that we may not even consciously share. Moreover, the comments we leave, the articles we share, and the groups we join create a trail of digital breadcrumbs that can be pieced together to reveal a more comprehensive picture of who we are online.

Layer 4: The Hidden Depths

IV. Identifying Unique Device Characteristics

Finally, beneath these visible layers lies a hidden depth: the unique characteristics of our devices. Hardware identifiers, operating system details, and even the way we interact with our devices can be used to create a profile that is virtually impossible to anonymize. This layer highlights the fact that our online identity isn't just about what we share; it's also about the tools we use and the ways we interact with them.

Understanding these layers of our online identity empowers us to make informed choices about our digital presence. By being aware of the data we generate and the ways it can be used, we can take control of our privacy and navigate the online world with greater autonomy and security.

CHAPTER 3
THE TOOLS AND TECHNIQUES
OF ONLINE ANONYMITY

The Tools and Techniques of Online Anonymity

our online activities leave a trail, making us vulnerable to tracking, surveillance, and data breaches. But fear not, fellow digital citizen! This chapter equips you with the tools and techniques to cloak your online presence and become a master of anonymity.

1. Masking Your IP Address and Location:

The first step to online anonymity is obscuring your digital footprint. Your IP address acts like your online fingerprint, revealing your location and potentially linking your activities to you. Here's how to break free from that digital leash:

- VPNs (Virtual Private Networks): Imagine a tunnel that encrypts your internet traffic and routes it through a server in another location. That's a VPN in a nutshell. Popular VPN providers like NordVPN and ExpressVPN offer robust encryption and global server networks, making you appear like a digital nomad in the cyber world.

2. The Onion Router of Anonymity:

TOR: Think of Tor as a maze of encrypted tunnels built by volunteers around the globe. Your data hops through these tunnels, bouncing off multiple nodes, making it nearly impossible to trace its origin. Tor is a powerful tool for researchers, journalists, and anyone seeking ultimate anonymity.

3. Secure Browsers:

Firefox, Brave, DuckDuckGo for Enhanced Privacy: Not all browsers are created equal. Ditch Chrome and embrace the privacy-focused trio: Firefox, Brave, and DuckDuckGo. These browsers block trackers, cookies, and unwanted ads, making it harder for third parties to monitor your online movements.

4. Privacy-Focused Search Engines:

DuckDuckGo, Startpage, Swisscows: Google may be the king of search, but it also tracks your every query. Opt for privacy-focused search engines like DuckDuckGo, Startpage, and Swisscows. These search engines don't store your data or personalize results, keeping your search history truly private.

5. Password Managers and Strong Authentication Protocols:

Your passwords are the keys to your online kingdom. Use a secure password manager like LastPass or 1Password to create strong, unique passwords for every account. And don't forget about two-factor authentication (2FA) – it adds an extra layer of security by requiring a second verification step beyond your password.

Remember, online anonymity is a journey, not a destination. These tools are your armor, but vigilance and awareness are your ultimate weapons. Stay informed about the latest threats and adapt your strategies accordingly. With the right tools and knowledge, you can navigate the digital landscape with confidence, leaving behind only a faint whisper of your online presence.

CHAPTER 4
IMPLEMENTING ANONYMITY IN PRACTICE

Implementing Anonymity in Practice

Implementing anonymity in practice has become a crucial skill. Protecting your data and activities from prying eyes requires more than just incognito mode. This chapter delves into essential steps for securing your device and operating system, the bedrock of your anonymous journey.

1. Securing Your Device and Operating System

While mainstream operating systems offer some privacy features, they often prioritize convenience and data collection over user privacy. Consider switching to privacy-focused operating systems like Tails or Whonix.

- **Tails:** This live-CD Linux distribution boots entirely from RAM, leaving no trace on your hard drive. It comes pre-loaded with privacy-focused tools like Tor and encryption software.

- **Whonix:** This virtual machine-based operating system runs within your existing operating system, creating a secure sandbox environment for anonymous browsing and activities.

2. Encryption: Your Data's Bodyguard

Encryption scrambles your data into an unreadable format, rendering it useless to unauthorized individuals. Imagine it as a locked vault for your sensitive information. Popular options include

- **Disk Encryption:** Encrypt your entire hard drive for comprehensive protection, using tools like VeraCrypt or BitLocker.
- **File Encryption:** Secure specific files like documents, photos, or emails with tools like Axcrypt or GnuPG.
- **Cloud Storage Encryption:** Encrypt data before uploading it to cloud services like Mega or Tresorit.

3. Disabling Data Collectors: Taming the Telemetry Beast

Modern devices and operating systems collect a shocking amount of data about your usage habits, location, and even keystrokes. To minimize this data trail, consider:

- **Disabling location services:** GPS and Wi-Fi can pinpoint your location. Restrict access only to trusted apps.
- **Reviewing privacy settings:** Most operating systems offer granular control over data collection. Disable

unnecessary features like voice assistants or personalized advertising.

- **Auditing your apps:** Check app permissions and revoke access to irrelevant data like your contacts or camera.

CHAPTER 5
ANONYMIZING YOUR ONLINE ACTIVITIES

Anonymizing Your Online Activities

privacy is a precious commodity. With every click and scroll, we leave a trail of digital breadcrumbs, exposing our online activities to governments, corporations, and even curious strangers. In this chapter, we'll delve into the world of online anonymity and equip you with tools and strategies to reclaim your digital privacy.

1. Browsing the Web Safely with Privacy Extensions and Tools:

Think of your browser as a window into the digital world. While convenient, it's often an uncurtained window, revealing your browsing habits to anyone peeking in. But fear not! A plethora of privacy extensions and tools can transform your browser into a fortress of anonymity.

- **Privacy-focused browsers:** Explore privacy-focused alternatives like Brave, DuckDuckGo, or Tor Browser that block trackers, cookies, and fingerprinting attempts.
- **Privacy extensions:** Enhance your existing browser with extensions like Privacy Badger, uBlock Origin, and NoScript that block malicious scripts and trackers.
- **VPNs:** Virtual Private Networks mask your IP address and encrypt your traffic, making it harder to track your online movements. However, be wary of free VPNs, as they may compromise your data for profit.
- **Search engine alternatives:** Google isn't your only option! Try privacy-focused search engines like DuckDuckGo or Startpage for unbiased results without

data tracking.

2. Anonymous Email and Messaging Services

Email and messaging services can be breeding grounds for data collection. But worry not, there are ways to communicate without compromising your identity. Consider these options:

- **ProtonMail and Tutanota:** These secure email providers offer end-to-end encryption and anonymous sign-up, preventing anyone from snooping on your messages and perfect for sensitive communication.

- **Signal and Telegram:** Signal (open-source) and Telegram (cloud-based) These two encrypted messaging apps prioritize privacy with features like disappearing messages and self-destructing media. Perfect for confidential conversations without the fear of digital footprints.

- **Burner email services:** For situations where temporary anonymity is key, services like Burner Mail and Mailinator provide disposable email addresses that self-destruct after use and avoid linking your identity to specific accounts.

3. Securely Accessing Social Media and Online Accounts

Social media and online accounts can be tempting targets for hackers and identity thieves. But with some precautions, you can maintain your online presence while keeping your data safe.

- **Strong passwords and two-factor authentication:** Use unique, complex passwords for every account and enable two-factor authentication wherever possible. This adds an extra layer of security to deter unauthorized access.

- **Privacy settings**: Review and adjust the privacy settings on your social media and online accounts. Limit who can see your information and minimize the data you share publicly.

- **Social media alternatives:** Consider using privacy-focused social media platforms like Mastodon and Diaspora, which offer decentralized networks and greater control over your data.

4. Utilizing Cryptocurrency for Anonymous Transactions

While not foolproof, cryptocurrency can offer a degree of anonymity for online transactions. However, proceed with caution and consider the following.

- **Understanding the risks:** Cryptocurrency transactions are not entirely anonymous and can be traced with sophisticated techniques. Research and understand the potential risks before making any financial decisions.
- **Choosing the right platform:** Not all cryptocurrencies are created equal. Bitcoin, while popular, is relatively transparent. Consider alternatives like Monero and Zcash, which offer enhanced anonymity features.
- **Staying informed:** The landscape of cryptocurrency and regulations is constantly evolving. Stay informed about the latest developments and utilize reputable exchanges and wallets to safeguard your investments.

CHAPTER 6
MAINTAINING ANONYMITY IN
THE REAL WORLD

Maintaining Anonymity in the Real World

1. Public Wi-Fi:

Free Wi-Fi at cafes and airports might seem like a blessing, but it can be a privacy nightmare. Unsecured networks are like open doors for hackers, allowing them to eavesdrop on your online activities and steal sensitive data.

- **Avoid public Wi-Fi for sensitive activities:** Banking, online shopping, and accessing personal accounts should be done on secure networks.
- **Embrace VPNs:** Virtual Private Networks encrypt your data, making it unreadable even for the most skilled snoop. Choose a reputable VPN provider with strong encryption protocols.
- **Tether to your phone:** If you must use public Wi-Fi, consider using your phone's mobile hotspot as a secure connection.

2. Mobile Maze:

Outsmarting Location Tracking. Our smartphones are loyal

companions, but they can also be location trackers in disguise. To keep your movements private.

- **Disable location services:** Turn off location services unless you need them for specific apps. Remember, Google Maps and ride-hailing apps track your every move.
- **Use privacy-focused apps:** Explore alternative browsers and messaging apps that prioritize user privacy and minimize data collection.
- **Invest in a Faraday cage:** This nifty device blocks your phone's signal, preventing it from transmitting your location data.

CHAPTER 7
ADVANCED TECHNIQUES AND CONSIDERATIONS

Advanced Techniques and Considerations

- **Complexity:** These techniques require a deeper understanding of internet protocols and security mechanisms. Be prepared to invest time in research and learning.

- **Trade-offs:** Increased anonymity often comes at the cost of convenience, performance, and security guarantees. Evaluate your needs and risk tolerance before using these tools.

- **Legality:** Certain tools and techniques may have legal implications depending on your jurisdiction. Research and comply with relevant laws.

- **Social Engineering:** Anonymity doesn't protect against social engineering attacks. Maintain responsible online behavior and be wary of scams and phishing attempts.

CHAPTER 8
ADVANCED ANONYMITY TOOLS
AND TECHNIQUES

Advanced Anonymity Tools and Techniques

deep drive into advanced anonymity tools and techniques.

1. Tor Bridges and Onion Services for Deeper Anonymity:

Tor, the anonymity champion, offers a robust network for routing your traffic through multiple relays, obscuring your origin. However, even Tor isn't foolproof. Enter Tor bridges: specialized relays that circumvent entry node surveillance, adding another layer of obscurity. Additionally, onion services, accessible only through Tor, provide hidden websites and services, further increasing your anonymity for sensitive communication and browsing.

2. Multi-Signature Wallets and Anonymization Mixers for Cryptocurrency Transactions:

Cryptocurrency transactions, while pseudonymous, aren't truly anonymous. Multi-signature wallets require multiple authorized parties to sign a transaction, adding a layer of security and obscuring the origin of funds. Anonymization mixers, on the other hand, pool and shuffle cryptocurrency, making it difficult to trace the source and destination of individual transactions. These tools, however, come with their own challenges and risks, requiring careful research and implementation.

- **Multi-signature wallets:** Imagine a bank vault with multiple keys. Multi-signature wallets require more than one authorized party to spend your funds, adding an extra layer of security and potentially obscuring ownership.
- **Anonymization mixers:** Think of them as laundromats for your cryptocurrency. Mixers blend your coins with others, making it difficult to trace their origin and destination. Use trusted mixers with proven reputations to avoid scams.

3. Virtual Machines and Secure Enclaves for Isolated Browsing:

Virtual machines (VMs) provide similar sandboxing capabilities, allowing you to run a separate operating system and applications, Secure enclaves, like Intel SGX and AMD SEV, offer isolated execution environments within your own system, protecting your data and activity from the rest of the operating system. further compartmentalizing your online activities.

Virtual machines (VMs): create a separate operating system environment within your existing system. This allows you to run applications or browse the web in a completely isolated environment, further minimizing the risk of tracking or malware infections.

Secure enclaves: are isolated environments within your operating system that offer enhanced security for sensitive activities. They can be used to run browsers or applications without exposing your entire system and data.

CHAPTER 9
THE FUTURE OF ONLINE ANONYMITY

The Future of Online Anonymity

The internet, once a Wild West of anonymity, is rapidly transforming into a panopticon of surveillance. Technological advancements like facial recognition, deepfakes, and pervasive data collection threaten to strip us bare in the digital realm. Yet, amidst this encroaching transparency, embers of hope flicker – privacy advocates raising their voices, regulations grappling with ethical complexities, and innovative solutions emerging to reclaim our right to anonymity. This chapter delves into these intricate threads, exploring the challenges and opportunities that shape the future of online anonymity.

1. Tech Titans and the Privacy Paradox:

Technological progress, a double-edged sword, has revolutionized our lives but also chipped away at our anonymity. Facial recognition algorithms embedded in smartphones unlock our devices and secure our homes, but they also fuel mass surveillance systems and empower authoritarian regimes. Social media platforms, havens for connection and expression, meticulously track our online movements, building detailed profiles for targeted advertising and manipulation. The very tools that promise convenience and security often come at the cost of our privacy.

2. Privacy Advocates: Champions of the Invisible:

In this ever-evolving landscape, privacy advocates stand as guardians of our digital shadows. They raise awareness about the insidious ways our data is exploited, push for stricter regulations, and develop alternative technologies that prioritize privacy by design. From organizations like the Electronic Frontier Foundation (EFF) to grassroots movements like Stop the Cyborg, these tireless champions fight to ensure that anonymity remains a fundamental right, not a privilege.

3. Regulations: The Uneasy Dance of Control and Freedom:

Governments, grappling with the complexities of data privacy, are increasingly enacting regulations to rein in the tech giants and protect citizens' digital rights. GDPR, CCPA, and other privacy laws aim to give individuals control over their data, but their effectiveness remains a point of debate. Balancing the need for security and innovation with the right to anonymity is a delicate dance, and the future of online privacy hinges on finding the right rhythm.

4. Building a More Secure and Anonymous Digital Future:

Despite the challenges, the future of online anonymity isn't without hope. Technologies like blockchain, decentralized applications (dApps), and privacy-preserving encryption algorithms offer promising avenues to reclaim control over our digital lives. Open-source platforms and encrypted communication tools, fueled by the spirit of collaboration and innovation, can empower individuals to navigate the digital world with greater anonymity.

CHAPTER 10
THE CHALLENGES AND RISKS
OF ONLINE ANONYMITY

The Challenges and Risks of Online Anonymity

While online anonymity offers a sense of freedom and protection, it's not without its challenges and risks. Before diving headfirst into the shadows of the web, it's crucial to understand the potential pitfalls and navigate them responsibly.

1. Legal Implications and Ethical Considerations:

- **Privacy vs. Security:** The very act of seeking anonymity can raise suspicion, prompting authorities to investigate your online activities. Striking a balance between privacy and security becomes paramount.
- **Misinformation and Disinformation:** Anonymity emboldens some to spread misinformation and disinformation with impunity, contributing to online toxicity and manipulation. Responsible anonymity requires self-regulation and adherence to ethical principles.
- **Cybercrime and Harassment:** The veil of anonymity can shield cybercriminals and online predators, making it easier for them to target unsuspecting individuals. Vigilance and awareness of these threats are essential.

2. Balancing Anonymity with Convenience and Functionality

- **Real-world limitations:** Many online services and platforms require real-world identification for verification or account creation, limiting the scope of true anonymity. Finding alternative solutions that prioritize both privacy and functionality becomes necessary.

- **Accessibility and user experience:** Anonymity tools can sometimes add complexity and friction to online interactions, hindering user experience. Striking a balance between anonymity and usability becomes crucial for long-term adoption.

- **Loss of trust and accountability:** In a world reliant on online interactions, complete anonymity can hinder building trust and accountability. Finding ways to maintain a degree of transparency while safeguarding privacy becomes essential.

3. Staying Up-to-Date with Evolving Threats and Techniques:

- **Technological advancements:** As technology evolves, so do the methods used to track and identify online users. Staying informed about emerging threats and adapting your anonymity strategies accordingly becomes crucial.

- **Social engineering and phishing:** Malicious actors constantly develop new social engineering and phishing techniques to compromise anonymity. Educating yourself about these tactics and practicing caution is essential.

- **Legislation and regulations:** The legal landscape surrounding online anonymity is constantly evolving. Keeping yourself informed about relevant legislation and regulations ensures you remain on the right side of the law.

CHAPTER 11
CASE STUDIES OF ONLINE ANONYMITY IN ACTION

Case Studies of Online Anonymity in Action

- **Whistleblowing:** Edward Snowden's use of Tor to expose NSA surveillance sparked global conversations about government overreach. We'll analyze how anonymity enabled him to share critical information without fear of reprisal.

- **Activism:** Anonymous hacktivist groups like Anonymous and LulzSec have used online anonymity to expose corporate corruption and champion social causes. We'll examine their tactics and the impact of their actions.

- **Creative Expression:** Anonymity empowers individuals to express themselves freely, from dissident writers in oppressive regimes to masked artists like Banksy. We'll explore how anonymity fuels creativity and challenges censorship.

- **Personal Safety:** Journalists in war zones and victims of domestic abuse often rely on anonymity to protect themselves. We'll discuss tools and techniques for safeguarding online identities in vulnerable situations.

- **Business & Finance:** Anonymity plays a role in online marketplaces like Bitcoin and dark web forums. We'll examine the potential benefits and challenges of anonymity in the realm of commerce and finance.

Conclusion

1. Emerge from the Shadows, Empowered and Anonymous

You've reached the end of your journey into the world of online incognito. Throughout this book, we've delved into the depths of digital anonymity, exploring the tools, techniques, and mindsets necessary to reclaim your privacy in the ever-evolving landscape of the internet.

As you close this book, remember that **anonymity is not about hiding**. It's about taking control of your digital footprint, crafting an online persona that reflects your true self on your terms. It's about **empowerment**, not isolation.

2. The skills you've acquired empower you to

- **Navigate the digital world with confidence:** You're now equipped with the knowledge to choose the right tools, configure your privacy settings effectively, and leave minimal traces of your online activity.

- **Engage authentically:** You can express yourself freely online without compromising your privacy or security. Participate in online communities, share your passions, and connect with like-minded individuals, all while maintaining a comfortable level of anonymity.

- **Protect yourself from harm:** You've learned valuable strategies to stay safe from online threats like malware, phishing scams, and identity theft. Your newfound anonymity safeguards you from unwanted attention and empowers you to make informed decisions about your online presence.

Remember, **anonymity is a journey, not a destination**. The digital landscape is constantly evolving, and new threats and challenges emerge every day. Embrace continuous learning, stay updated on the latest privacy trends, and adapt your strategies accordingly.

As you step back into the online world, do so with a newfound sense of **freedom and control**. You are no longer a passive observer, but an active participant, shaping your digital identity with intention and purpose.

Go forth, **incognito warrior**, and reclaim your privacy. May your online journey be one of exploration, connection, and empowerment, always shrouded in the cloak of anonymity.

Beyond the Book:

Your journey into online anonymity doesn't end with the last page. Here are some additional resources to keep you informed and empowered

- **Privacy-focused news websites:** Stay updated on the latest privacy news and developments with websites like The Privacy Blog, Restore Privacy, and Electronic Frontier Foundation.
- **Online communities:** Join online forums and communities dedicated to privacy and anonymity, such as r/privacy, r/privacytoolsIO, and Anonymity subreddit.
- **Privacy-focused tools and services:** Explore and experiment with the ever-growing range of privacy-focused tools and services available, from secure browsers and search engines to encrypted messaging apps and virtual private networks.

Remember, the key to online anonymity is **constant vigilance and adaptation**. By staying informed, engaged, and adaptable, you can confidently navigate the digital world with your privacy intact.